EL BILINGUAL CATARSIS

EL BILINGUAL CATARSIS

A Collection of Poetry

Wendy Avilés

NEW DEGREE PRESS
COPYRIGHT © 2022 WENDY AVILÉS
All rights reserved.

EL BILINGUAL CATARSIS
A Collection of Poetry

ISBN
979-8-88504-909-2 *Paperback*
979-8-88504-780-7 *Kindle Ebook*
979-8-88504-259-8 *Digital Ebook*

This is for every person that inspired, supported, and believed in me. My appreciation for your time is absolute, and this collection is also dedicated to you, who motivated me to sit down and finally put it all together to publish.

CONTENTS

	NOTE FROM THE AUTHOR	9
CHAPTER 1	XVI	17
CHAPTER 2	XVII	25
CHAPTER 3	SECOND-WORST, YET TRANSFORMATIONAL	31
CHAPTER 4	SE PUEDE	43
CHAPTER 5	QUARANTIME	63
CHAPTER 6	XXI	73
	ACKNOWLEDGMENTS	83
	APPENDIX	89

Note from the Author

"If there is any kind of magic in this world, it must be in the attempt of understanding someone, sharing something."
— CELINE, *BEFORE SUNRISE*

"Necesitamos dar descanso a la lengua nombrada minorizada para que podamos de manera más urgente, y más efectiva, abogar a favor de los hablantes minorizados."

"[...] las lenguas no están aisladas, identificadas o definidas en términos léxico-estructurales. Más bien se establecen sobre la base de la identidad y la historia compartida de personas que hablan idiolectos diferentes pero parcialmente superpuestos que, por convención, y sólo cuando se dan ciertas condiciones sociales e históricas, se reúnen bajo un único rótulo lingüístico."
— OFELIA ET AL. (2015)

Between Santo Domingo and Atlanta, I've been writing verses as a way to cope with change. It's hard to encapsulate within a single or even multiple sentences the inevitable strikes of humaneness that fill us up or break us apart. Poetry is vulnerability—putting your bare face in the eyes of the public, an audience filled with people that know you, and also those who don't. Sharing your creative, transparent, heavy emotional work is also hard, especially the first time.

Billy Collins, former US Poet Laureate (2001-2003), said in his MasterClass that "poetry is the only full history we have of the human heart." More than that, he also described it as "a way of seeing life and establishing a connection to the world." For me, writing poetry is, in the simplest terms, a way to cope with the day to day in a creative fashion—a form of *catarsis*. In that process, I believe poets leave pieces of their reality, through imagery, especially intentions and emotions, on paper for others to glimpse their most vulnerable and analytical side. Poetry, then, becomes a testament of important or meaningful little and big moments in life (from skydiving to sitting in my room hoping for more during quarantine), without having to linearly place and condition it on the limitations of prose.

My desire with *El Bilingual Catarsis*, my first poetic memoir, is to simply create and share for the sake of honoring the art form. Hopefully, by doing so, I can contribute to the world of poetry, whether that involves a new style or structure, a different metaphor or imagery, or merely sparking some feeling in a stranger. Secondly, I aim to express my experience as a college student, latina, technically linguist but definitely bilingual, hoping that somebody else sees my effort as a way to make representation of those communities visible and highlight our role, particularly in the intersection of two worlds.

As an author, I look forward to initiating conversations with readers, starting with this collection; to engage in dialogue about crucial topics regarding human identity. Creative writing, then, becomes a tool for me to productively deliver a nonconformist position on language, as it is not only a system of communication but also one to both subconsciously and consciously project and determine our identity and loyalty to the communities we grew up in. My community originates in Santo Domingo, the capital of the Dominican Republic.

This collection has a peculiarity: it's bilingual. In some poems, you will also notice that while one of the two languages will dominate, the other will still be present, or you may even see a case of Spanglish. To me, growing up bilingual, translating thoughts on the spot did not come naturally, yet code-switching did. For this reason, you will mostly see code-switching in full sentences or independent clauses, with some exceptions, since writing requires more concentration and awareness than spoken language (thus, the other more complex ways of code-switching might not be as prominent here than those found in oral communication).

As stipulated by Juan Flores (1945), code-switching serves as "an alternative form of resistance, not a deliberate ignorance of multicultural realities but a different and potentially more democratic way of apprehending them." With this, speakers of Spanglish, like me, continually touch base at the intersection of their linguistic identities. For many, Spanglish often becomes a source of embarrassment instead of pride, but if there's anything that I would want you to take from this collection, even if it's not a new image or metaphor, it is that being part of *transculturación* doesn't have to be shameful. While there are contexts for different forms of writing and speaking, leading to informal or formal discourse, to repress expressing yourself in a pure way with other bilinguals based on standard language ideology would be an imposition on your personal identity.

Over fifty years ago, Einar Haugen (1966) explained how the term 'dialect' typically suggests informal or lower-class or rural speech (342). Standard language ideology makes us believe that only the standard language is the correct form of expression, which is, for most societies, the language of the upper classes, automatically established as a fixed political and pedagogic tool. Haugen held that "nation and language have become inextricably intertwined," and the "national ideal demands that there be a single linguistic code by means of which this communication can take place." The dialect, then, is "potentially disruptive to a unified nation," especially if those who teach languages are not part of the expected standard (345).

I read somewhere once that an 'ideal' is by definition something that can never be found; these will never go beyond being "ideals," considering that within a nation, dialects will always exist because individuals build solidarity to linguistic elements that represent characteristics of their community, many times without realizing it! (Quick proof: how many times have you heard somebody say that they don't have an accent?) While *national* loyalty could be in accordance with a standard language, this ideology creates an imaginary bridge between the different communities that adopt that language and, with evolution and points of contact, this would still diverge into dialects. All of this does *not* mean I am against standardization necessarily since Spanish (or French, or English) has overwhelming advantages, like easing communication in environments such as the workplace, but it somewhat symbolizes "past oppression and conveys an alien culture" (346). Just imagine the Dominican Republic without all the dominicanisms and the lexical and phrasal varieties that stand out and represent our culture (baltrí, fukú, teteo, etc.), or the Latin American ones for that matter.

Going back into poetry, just like code-switching "makes sense" to bilinguals, verses just ache to come out of a poet's mind. As I started to explain before, putting together a collection to share depths of thoughts—which I possibly haven't even shown to some of my closest people—is not inherently natural. In 2019, after multiple emotional turning points in my life, including my first romantic breakup and the passing of my grandfather, Justo Avilés, I reached the peak of my writing in terms of quantity. This continued up until 2020, when the pandemic brought me into a few writing blocks, finding it hard to get inspired by solely looking at my four walls.

However, even before the pandemic began playing a leading role in my early twenties, imposter syndrome started to diminish my aspirations to become a published writer. Insecurity in my ability to put my best work out there made me question why anybody should be reading my poems when there are countless masterpieces available to the public eye. Now, I believe I must take the necessary steps to act according to what I have preached; the extraordinary thing about writing poetry is sharing the tangible and intangible compelling details that shriek to be disclosed. And, even if this is merely my first official attempt to publicize my writings and I expect the skill to become more polished with time, the poems—as they stand today—are the most genuine version of my experiences that I can bring you at this point in time.

Traveling back and forth from Atlanta to Santo Domingo as an international student, I have faced linguistic and cultural challenges that have shaped not only my perspective of the world, but also my writing. With the most predominant themes of the collection being love, anxiety to accomplish and perfect, politics and questioning tradition, and body image, I've organized the book chronologically, so that you can follow some of the moments when I have decided to resort to writing as a main coping mechanism to explore desires, thoughts, and sensory experiences. Thus, each chapter equates to a year in my life, up until 2021.

No matter at what point in *your* life you're at, I'm eternally grateful you're joining me at this stage in mine. This is where the linguistic and creative dialogue begins.

Atentamente, y con muchísimo agradecimiento,
Wendy Avilés

CHAPTER 1

XVI

6:15 A.M.

Sonó la alarma.
Ha sido todo un engaño.
Él vivía en la noche,
soñaba en el día.

Vi a mi similar—
misma sangre, rostro decaído.
¡Qué pesadilla!
¿Así se siente?

Conozco gente así;
Todo les resbala,
nada les pica...
Es ahogarse en desdicha.

Hermano mío, ¡Reacciona!
Comprende que aquí
el valor trasciende
lo que la mente cosecha.

BEEP. BEEP.
Betrayal.
Became, him, alive at night,
                          dreamt daytime.

Bathed in Ghost mode:
same blood, decayed expression.
Bitter nightmare.

Reckless indifference,

                          drowning misery.

Brother, snap out of it!
                          Here,
our value transcends
what the mind harvests.

The Highest Level of Math Is Standard

These

   raindrops

      are desperately   seeking change

    frustrated with

        whiteness of white boards

bleeding through

        equations on blank paper,

  wishing

      they could

erase

the loneliness

and

be more than

less than

standard.

(Reasonable) Sacrifice

/ˈsakrɪfʌɪs/

    to choose which lamb to slaughter
            which plant to water
            which road to follow
            which language to write the poem in
            which future deserves fruition
            which project to finish
            which alternative is reliable
            which life to be remembered
            which life to be remembered

¿Ilusiones Pasajeras?

Miro al cielo, no me quejo;
lo que necesito, lo tengo.
¿Será real la reflexión en agua
si cuando la alcanzas desaparece?

No hay peor desdicha que
ilusionarme y desvanezcas.
Demuéstrame que en tu corazón
habita lo que en el mío falta.

CHAPTER 2

XVII

En Diagonal

Horizontal o vertical,
se mantiene igual.
Me muevo de aquí allá
buscando lo que me incline
en
    diagonal.

La alarma y el calendario
conspiran contra mi ánimo.
En la sacudida de los días,
sin defensa.

Sigo en la vuelta
buscando ser
encontrada por quien
me tiene enfrente.

Aquí estoy
sin fuerzas
pero
    estoy.

Desesperación Del Radio Público

Fuera de la ventana,
se escuchaban los pasos y
los pitos de aliento en vano.

Con amor interminable,
en sus frentes,
la bandera tricolor.

En el radio y en la calle,
el disgusto colectivo
pintado de verde fe.

Soñaban con despertarse
con el arduo trabajo
de posiciones bien asumidas.

Allá fuera, mi loco,
ta' marchando un bollue gente
en cacerolazo y gritando el maso.

Con pila 'e pique
y el verdadero caloraso
hondean la bandera.

En to' lo' stories uno ve
la gente tirá, entregá,
todito' de verde.

¿Hasta cuándo e'
que van a segui'
robando?

Revelación de Miradas

No quería mirarte,

No debía mirarte;

Me leerías la palma;

con la mirada, entenderías.

Con la mirada, trazarías

la línea de la vida.

Sabía que olvidaría la desdicha

de no verte,

de no sentirte.

yet I did.

I didn't owe it to you.

Easy to decipher?

To you. With a glance

you freely dance across my palm,

pointing out my life line.

Your absence

                no longer

                        was.

3
Second-Worst, Yet Transformational

Azul Es Mi Color

I.
Nací en la sombra de
las hojas de palmeras
con vista al cielo azul.

II.
Crecí con terror al misterio
y al inesperado empuje
del hondo Mar Caribe.

III.
Me acostumbré al invierno tropical,
ver mi madre recibir rosas de
relucientes pétalos tintados.

IV.
Pregunté innumerables veces
el preferido tono del océano a
mis similares; nunca cambia.

V.
Conocí al ladrón de la mitad de
mi identidad; admiraba sus
escritos de tinta azulada.

VI.
Asisto días de semana, esperando
una señal de vida, esperando
caer, y seguir cayendo

en tus aros verdes
con azul.

Time, I—

1.
Tick-tock,
tick-tock,

tick—as I look at
the hands of the clock. Seems that
these indicate time for everyone
else. For me, these point out the

loss of time—time I
could have invested. They're
waiting.

Time, I have wasted, contemplating
the petals that fell,
the numbers I could have raised.

I look at my hands; they
give me nothing but
the wrinkly yellow undertones of what
are supposed to serve as signs

of the fruits I have been,
or could have been,
harvesting.

2.
Yet. It. Passes… I heard them
ticking. That's all they ever do—
they invade the nerve that
drives me to go

beyond what
they
  try
    to
      prove.

Limit.

I *tap, tap,*
tap my feet. Perhaps to find,
to understand, to imitate the rhythms
created desperately
to provide, to act how
the hands, empty hands,
should.

Tap, tick-tock,
my pen swings from east to west.

Individual parts of my body shake
to get the answers,
the signs,
the measures to fulfill.

Up ahead the hands of the clock,
down, the bouncy feet,
with me, the empty, incomplete hands,
  once
    again.

3.
Noises thought as recognizable
conspire against
the consciousness that
agitates for a well-constructed face.

The echoing chatter and
the coffee stains alert me that
as more time goes by,
the less dust in my hands remains.

Tick tick tick...
I'm moving backward,
away from the currents.
I close my eyes.

Time
   to
      stop

    watching

the clock.

Shyness or Despicable Minds

Is my spirit a repellent
to fiends in a pretty suit?

Is my aura distancing
charm and care?

Collateral interventions:
do these improve the situation?

Spicy looks and shine—
isn't it all a cover-up?

Shyness or despicable minds...
maybe just the latter.

Wear Not-Too-Dark Sunglasses

It's one of those days.
The sun's short wavelengths
encourage you to
match its energy.

First day of the
plainly glottal week ahead.
No expectations other than
rowing your way.

Then, the heavy shadow—
tunnel view filter—
comes with futile shaking
for clarity.

Shadow dragged you
around like a *trapo*, and
comes back to
disrupt your chill, again.

Acts like it never leaves—
remains to actively hold back
when you've felt you're
no longer carried around.

Avoidant, you run.

You let ambiance
take your reality and
twist it into a better one.

Yet,

for the first time,
sunlight fails. Defeated.
Once again, useless.

For the first time,
shutting out the light
is no headache.

And, yet,

one act of "I see you"
ignites the light
within.

Stop Begging

Stop begging the waves
to move your way.

Stop asking the breeze
to refresh your steps.

Stop chasing rays
to shine on your face.

Stop forcing them
to stay.

Hoy Decidí Hacerle Caso a Las Olas

Las olas del viento, las olas del mar—
todas me llaman y me empujan
a cantar, bailar, desear un
nuevo corazón. Uno que se
moldea al alma refrescada.

Perseguía una fuerte brisa.
Prometía esperanzas, claveles,
frutos de otra vida. Vida pasada—
cáscara negra de guineo—
me encaminó a un ramo nuevo.

De momento a otro, nace una cara
diferente, pero aún joven. Corrientes
con distintas temperaturas, pero
un destino. Uno extraño, aunque
con sentido... chocante.

No lo veía; fue repentino.
Aunque con moratones,
si la divina comedia quiero,
evolucionar, absolver debo
lo que me brindan las olas.

4

Se Puede

PROLOGUE TO CHAPTER 4

"Are you sad?" asked the massage therapist, breaking the silence for the first time, forty minutes into the appointment. Her question completely caught me off guard. Without much thought, I shook my head and asked what made her think that; she remained quiet until the end of the session.

As soon as she finished, she questioned me again. This time, the lady asked where I live and whether it's a cold place. At first, I had no idea where she was going with this. I found these questions oddly specific since the woman didn't even know my name. I told her I am originally Dominican but studying somewhere else, and that the place could be colder than the Dominican Republic. The lady nodded.

After a short pause, she revealed that the reason she asked if I was sad was she believed—based on her former practices and studies—emotions are mostly concentrated around the hip area. Therefore, whenever she got close to that area while massaging me, she was expecting me (like any other person) to give some sign of life.

The lady continued, this time confidently saying: "You know exactly what you want, and you are not afraid to get it. My only concern is that you lack an emotional response. Your emotions are deeply hidden." Her comment struck me; it was as if she had known me for years.

She decided I needed a hot tea and, noticing that I had a subungual hematoma (that I caused myself by accidentally smashing my thumb as I violently closed the car door), added, "By the way, the accident with your finger wasn't really an accident. The left side symbolizes heaven and the right side symbolizes the world. You were angry at the world when it happened." I felt quite unsettled. I thanked her.

¿Qué Es Poesía?

Completando lo empezado por Bécquer (Rima XXI).

Un grito al viento,
un suspiro en el intento,
un momento infinito...

¿Qué es poesía? ¿Y tú me lo preguntas?
eso, también, es poesía.

I Don't Plagiarize

Avilés. (2019). *I'm Trying Not to Plagiarize,*
    But Not Even This Piece Is Mine.
    Do you comment on the world,
    or, do you create your own?

Avilés. (2019). *Are Your Sentences a Creation from Innovation?*
    Because, allow me to find validation:
    "To know what a sentence means is to know its truth
    conditions—what the world must be like to be true."

Avilés. (2019). *Did You Write It Down,*
    and Memorize It?
    Cite my copy-paste,
    or put a hashtag on it.

Avilés. (2019). *My Roses Are Blue,*
    Your Violets Are Red.
    The poet's life begins
    when they're dead.

Avilés. (2019). *Post My Poems*
    in Your Insta Story!
    Perhaps I'll get reposted.
    Perhaps I'll get more followers.

Avilés. (2019). *Citational Anxiety Ain't a Thing*
    When You're Willing to Think.
    I'm a scholar, don't u C?
    I write GREAT verses. I repeat.

Avilés. (2019). *WTF Is a Hyperbole?*
    Pass me the dictionary.
    I'll include some terminology,
    but especially the bibliography.

Avilés. (2019). *I Write Masterpieces.*
    W. B. Yeats would agree
    with me. With
    writing, responsibility.*

*And, with responsibility, a writer's shine begins.

The Loop of Another Quiet Space

Confined, no cessation of palpitations.
    No script nor score. I hear beyond.
Each exhale accelerates the drums.
The dust settles. Stiffened,
my limbs are like pale sticks.

Fresh bread personified the room:
    tables packed with papers.
On the window: rain or smoke?
Commas, quotes, periods on hold,
skipping sheets in the Almond Blossom journal.

Still, pretending that I had planned out,
    I'm trapped by the bulbs and bound to the chair.
"Do something! Start working, Black Coffee!"
My pencil like eraser, my email bombarded by strangers.
I attempt to remove my feet from the invisible chains.

I *tried* to revive my strength.
    Body disengaged.
I fall under. My hand touches the wall,
encapsulated as though my mind had
become a string now tied into a knot.

Pulled this way, and by the tension
    ahead, I could fake a *try*—
a placebo across the gray atmosphere
like new iPhones replicating
genius-like proposals of development.

Kindles gathered around the corners, and
   in the center, notebooks closed.
A bookmark ripped in two, now there is
not so little inspiration. I move nervously,
releasing, but not ridiculously for attention.

My legs stretch below. Sticks hoping to
   find some warmth. Toes navigate
the mattress, fingers guide
the pen barrel, and I
slide my hand across the tabletop.

Bent over, performing the thoughts, my glasses
   record the awaited response.
I write a sentence,
         sliding,

             painting a landscape,
then moving away to break the
subconscious, agonizing habit. The wait

brings no signs. There's no timer at twenty-minute
   intervals to resolve my strife.
The lights stare: shush, hush, conflicted workaholics
with familiar faces. A frown appears upon mine.
"Embrace the attempt!" the wall claims.

Overlooking the landscape, I appreciate the disorganization.
   Fueled by the likes, an invention
with notifications. Yet, in an instant, unresponsiveness.
The firmer I seem, the more unbothered I become.
And yet, I begin to hear the palpitation again.

La Razón Contra la Emoción: Una Reflexión

Porque dentro de mí siempre estuvo. La misma intensidad que en un momento pareció chocante, electrificante, y hasta irrazonable, se mantuvo.

En la búsqueda de un refugio que pueda soportar tanta pasión, creando un miedo eterno por algún día perderlo, me empujó a construir las mismas paredes que me impidieron verla. Me cerraron en la oscuridad confusa que intentaron convencerme por innumerables días de que ellas harían el trabajo, y que por esto, podría imaginarme una vida sin amor—momentáneamente.

Peor oscuridad, que la que te ofrece un puente de oportunidades para luego apuñalarte con la realidad solitaria, no existe.

Quería convertir el polvo de las paredes en caminos para viajes con cosechas independientes, y obras que reconozcan un talento surgido de una única fuente. Lo más decepcionante es que la gran lógica con la cual ellas me llenaban de esperanzas no era más que otra imagen, otra fantasía, porque en la ruta que me encontraba trotando—aunque no perfecta—era la que me convenía.

Las paredes no me advirtieron que, para llegar a un destino como el que me pintaban, iba a tener que recorrer caminos estrechos de amores insatisfactorios; el mundo no es para vivirlo en solitario.

La razón guiada por la emoción era la más completa. Me lo advirtieron algunos pasajeros: el propósito recae en el amor y la conexión.

La vida te entrega consecuencias de lo que fríamente planeas (*me jodí*).

Así de gris es la corriente.

Would You Draw Me?

Thursday, 2:29:55 p.m.
Shiny oak oval table chiseled
by exhales; it's the prompt.

In front, still:
you, your iPad and stylus;
then, professor and lesson.

Warm, grainy floor below,
two spots, dark chairs.
I picked the farthest.

Two feet away, I attempt to climb
your notes. I spread
like slime through

the room,
           a moment suspended,

repeated each week,
when our routines meet.
The class of shining eyes

to the Italian architecture
you sketched in strikes.

Going Greek in 2019:
A First Impression

One shot. Come meet us!
We're as cool as Saturdays at 1 a.m.
when we puked the vodka sour
after our date party—no scam.

                         (Just don't mention the bar.)

Two sisters whisper,
another rants.
Can you tell the difference?
I *genuinely* can't.

                         (Boys bring drama.)

Three heads, a conversation
recited like prayer.
Remember, the discretion:
"Our Father in Heaven" air.

                         (Attract? the PNMs.)

High-pitched Vitruvian women
scatter in white cotton tops.
Wine stained images
harm the flock.

                         (Zero Booze in photos!)

Ice cubes in a mold:
excuse for some tags.
Behold!
A feature for the Gram!

                         (Worth the dues?)

Okay, you're finally cool
that you committed to this.
You're set for undergrad.
Congrats, sis!

Placards and Ties

Glares intertwine,
not once nor twice.
Breaths ignite:
it's you and I,

months behind.
Placards and ties—
I disguised
gin shots, an Uber ride.

In waves you came,
but you never stayed.
You remained,
but you never stayed.

Merging blocs,
and blocks away,
but gin again:
I hoped for

your face, or a text.
A sign to rewind,
finish the race.
And then,

the then.
Then pushed,
then danced.
Swam in crowds

to find.

I Wanna Know Your Name

I don't do some times, some days.
You're either in fully, or you better
        leave.

        It's not whenever you're "feeling it."
        I might love mangos, but I'm
        certainly not a mango tree.
        I'm not a flower that you can
        pick and use for the festivity.
        I'm not data in your experiment.

I want real conversations. I am
curious—I am interested in those
lively peculiar details that make
your stomach sick, or sore. I wanna
know what moves you, what strikes
you. I want you to share the smallest
objectives you've set. I want to
cry your distress, celebrate your
success. I want to be as yours
as you are to yourself. I just want
to be important, and so you tell.

I am reliable pain. I am confused
innocence. I am the touch you
don't grasp. I am the love you
don't take. I am the smiles you
don't admit exist. You resist.

And all I ask for is to know your name.
So you say I exaggerate.

We just don't see the same way, thus
I gotta give myself some credit. I'll
greet you in heaven—
>	*if you ever accept it.*

Se Buscan Almas

Las fiestas no son para
el ron y la sed de pérdida,
sino quienes se unen y
crean armonía.

Una orquesta no se compone
de quienes tocan solos su instrumento.
Es de quienes disfrutan de
un espectáculo colectivo.

Se buscan almas que deseen
ser una. La fiesta de la vida
no se disfruta en solitario.

Encuéntrame

Encuéntrame en cada partícula,
                        átomo,
                        célula.
Encuéntrame en cada discusión
      con armas disfuncionales.
Encuéntrame en cada estrofa,
                        verso,
                        palabra,
                        sílaba.
Encuéntrame en lo que se mueve
               por discomfort.
Encuéntrame en lo que se esconde
      de las olas en marea
                        alta.
Encuéntrame en lo que ves pero
               no aprovechas.
      En lo que recuerdas pero
               no retomas.
Encuéntrame en lo que se descifra
      en sistemas de signos.
Encuéntrame en lo que estuvo a tu alcance
                    no más.
Encuéntrame en lo que no espera,
      no (quiere) busca(r).
Encuéntrame para así
             encontrarte, por fin.

No Soy Tu Medicina

No me necesitas para curarte.
No estoy aquí como un escape,
como una loción anti-amargues.

Si esperas que me transforma,
si esperas que de repente sea
lo que ni tú entiendes que se arregla,

no me uses.
No me uses como la salida
de tus paredes de cera.

Hay bastante que ofrecer
y por tus piedras huecas
no me hundo en pleno amanecer.

Para algo hay tanta variedad
en el mar—le sobran
misterios que explorar.

another contemporary poem on identity

my linguistics professor says
you can't learn a language
without having a conversation
with a native speaker.

you have to survive,
try to survive.

writer. linguist. astronaut.
mathematician. politician.
teacher. psychologist. You?

no, I, I go with the breeze,
with the waves.
i'm the color of the sea—
wait.

but, today, 100 percent in le composition.
c'est le intermediate French,
mais, je ne sais pas encore
poser des questions.

do you know
where to go
with a minor in French,
with a minor in LING?

gotta practice,
talk experience.

liberal arts degree
will set me free:
multiple paths—
liberté indeed!

my career in America:
blue identity,
red intensity.
soy Latina.

Aislada

Fall 2019, second year.
December 12th is setting,
a few days before departure.

Watery warmth glinting.
WOODRUFF HALL.
I push the door, I'm back.

Sea of white sheets: I'm wrapped.
I turn around while I lie,
waves of another hectic day.

I'm carried away
with ticking in my chest
and papers on my bed.

The sheets are spread,
the silhouette by my side.
In palm trees I confide.

No deadlines, no clocks.
No impending masks…
my island, I fantasize.

5
Quarantime

When?

When I am back on the road,
when the window is half-closed,
when in the reflection a contrast
between my brown, your green.

When the limbs get cold,
when the smirk is alone,
and when it's gone, the Snap is too—
a fantasy sustained, a notification retained.

The world we live in: a polaroid in red,
the screen of a (not) new decade, or
the twentieth scare of cooperation and
the twentieth love of indignation.

In My Room

The tropical warmth of the breeze
dances, pushes my window, wipes
its sweat of temperature change,
whispering your name.

The corners of the desolated bedroom
collect the dust, glancing at the dates
to wait for, at the Clorox that led them on,
at the second 42-min call to move the ATL flight.

The AC does its best, relying on a wall
that has heard the "SET ME FREE" green
playlist as I tap away from "Quarantine,"
peak of Disney closing its doors—history.

And in micro-history, I slide through the
two (but singular) photos on my iPad,
and I, hoping for a two-person quarantine,
instead found myself imprisoned.

Too Much Time

I spend too much time
waiting for things to occur.
Will my thighs continue to
grow in the midst of no lure?

Nails like swings,
hairs' height almost mine,
and still no vaccine to suffice,
no magic soap to terminate strife.

The drops in the sink imitate *tick-tock*,
but *tick-tock* no more tells time.
Where do we look for a sign?

What Moves Their Way and Stays?

Ten times a day, I wonder
what moves their way and stays;
what keeps their glance unshaken,
what drives them to the wait.

As fishers fish for hours
and boats find a bay,
young boys drop the towel
for a verse they can't retain.

subject: what if we

what if i told you there is a way. an option the Christian moms would frown upon at noon after they drop their kids at school, yet binge novelas on. what if i told you your suspicions are true, and not only have you been right, but also the cause is you, too. what if i told you I want a pause of storyline, time.
    would you guide me to get lost, and then to find?
             will i find, or wait again—every three seasons—for the sync in doubt?
    what if i told you this could be correct; not in their terms, but to put a foot down in this roundabout. what if i told you no matter how long the clock ticks away, when the sixth or seventh month is back, so will we land under the same sun and reclaim our roots, alive.
    what if i told you i could guide you too, multiplying what has drawn me to the cause. what if i told you i could compromise, so we can seal the envelope, and mail it to open later. what if you send me a handwritten letter, you know, those that push your stomach to play sick and yack words today you would otherwise not let go. what if this is mine, and i'm hoping you are fine. what if we—
    i'm looking forward to your response...
                                if you ever (re)read it.

I Wonder

I do wonder oftentimes—no,
   I wonder   all   the   Time
   got us   still, handwritten
once, twice, thrice. María
stares, wrapped in aluminum,
an almost-scratch in agenda.
She comforts me with jazz, or
lo-fi silhouette   6:0789 p.m.,
and I'm back.   Here, in waves,
the dream of return—   is?
Bouncing, and then, laid Pink
Skies, and down to yoga mat.
I can work out, but six is my max.
   Do you, *Unmasked,*   ever feel
it too? The s t r e t c h of reality
   we   push up   through?
Push up. I'm impenetrable outside.
   I—   push up   The ceiling ain't the
   sky.   push up   Breathing is cleaner
   inside. Don't   push up   lose the streak.
   Our choices are three, but   push up
   one   stop   is what we need.
Do not become the enemy.

Skydi(v)e

Autopilot, but [free]falling,
hoping, fourteen thousand feet above
above would be brighter.

But, brighter is the ground, impacted.
Brighter is the 120 mph pressure—silence.
Brighter is the third Atlanta power outage.

Brighter is the dry oatmeal;
I'm ill—blue without the berry.
Another one in the pandemic:

no COVID-19, just 2020.

Pale Blue Eyes - The Velvet Underground

En mis tímpanos, sus latidos,
minimizando las letras del título—
serán prohibidos sus Pálidos Ojos Azules.

Nueva vez, viejo patrón disolvente.
Frío de noche Carolina del Norte,
huyéndole a las ramas húmedas.

Luna escondida por algodón,
y alma encendida, abrazada:
no hay más triste fortaleza.

¿Cuánto durará… la vida del fósforo,
condenada a quemar mis dedos?

6
XXI

Puddle by Puddle

I knock the door—
I guess I'm home.
The palm trees softly kneel
at my entrance. My brother,

with his hands on his hips,　　　　"¿será que otra ve' en teteo?"
shaking his head, questions.　　　(yes, teteo made it into a
Right pass him, as if two　　　　　poetry collection)
Ubers in traffic, without

looking back, I'm back
at my sanctuary. Tonight,
it's not good enough.
Seems I must knock

on the master bedroom.
Must report on the current　　　　dique pa' que no se quillen
events, and the future too.
But, the weather and green

I can't predict. I, I'm
going puddle by puddle.
Despite the blocks,
I'll find gold, then...　　　　　　nama si Dios quiere

Tumultuous

I prayed for moments like these,
yet my mind isn't at ease. You,

who reflects the complementary, unafraid.
Who spills red and green, yellow and purple
on my white and black—no neutral, contrast.

I mentioned consumption of my workaholic self,
but that's been your strategy. You,

who drives back every two days.
Who writes of sunny shroom trips,
with silver and gold rings, and golden mid-forehead split.

The mix is tumultuous.
The outcome: permanent, filling.

I can't come back from what you've taught me.

Still

Yoga mat still stretched.
Tea bag still soaked.
So are the veggies still,
waiting on the plate,
drowned by unfiltered
sink water.

Simple to have motivation
before sweating energy.
Simple to enjoy salad
when honey makes the mix.
Simple to make promises
before meeting Defeat.

Sometimes I Confuse Black with White

Sounds stupid, but black can blend with white,
and it's not grey I see. Sometimes the canvas is
white to remain; sometimes it's more than base.

Sometimes fluid white doesn't reflect, but projects
what must be ~~erased~~ covered, to then
sketch and release the idyllic image.

Sometimes underpainting *is* the move. Sometimes a
verse without rhyme holds purer truth. Sometimes I
confuse feeling with planning—against morality.

See, philosophers argue one is good through service,
when putting others first. Does it matter, when
therapists claim courage is key, and self-care is peaking?

Underpainting is expensive. Self-care is too when catching
flights for service to survive distance, to resume a
(love) language: your painting. Sometimes I wonder if

I'm still the artist. The black looks nicer in my eyes, but
does it matter if my perspective is known to be selfish?
Sometimes, we hold too dear justifications for the white.

I Didn't Want to Shut You Down

Grasping my hand, you asked to be included,
to activate the side of me that was off. I thought

it was a simple Sunday stroll after 1 p.m. French toasts.
Nothing about Prospect Park suggested I needed help. Earlier,

nothing about dancing while seated as I celebrated a cheat meal,
or taking a photo of blueberries, whipped cream, and maple syrup

asked to be assisted, to be heard, to be approached with logic.
For me, it has all been thought through, or so I thought.

I thought one dessert max each vacation day with 20k steps.
I thought every piss and shower required a mirror check.

You held onto me—shook me to challenge the strict rules, yet
ruling me, claiming no agency, a "fuck you" was my gift.

A Heartbreak Isn't an External Invitation

para Maiah y Paola

Snapping me out of it
without shaking my shoulders:
you've got no arms left.

Stories of shit-talking cloud
your head as if it's a word
problem. I'm not good at math

either—no surprises here.
Though, it can't be clearer:
you extend a silver plate,

they hand you rocks.
Should you hold,
and for how much longer?

Your arms are not suitcases
and yet you're carrying.
Every second you hope

an asshole has good motive,
you're still crushed, becoming
                    unrecognizable.

De Otra, No Me Queda

No me queda más que la nostalgia
de olas contra el borde abismal,
de luna salpicada en Mar Caribe,
de asiento delantero, pero pasajero.

De otra, no me queda más que
la mirada flotante buscando encajar,
de ayuno alargado, de meses en vano,
de tu mano sobre la mía, como rutina.

for the proud majority who doesn't like poetry

they say having a lot of red marks
on a paper is a tough spot, but then
why did my poetry professor only
mark-up the outstanding experiments?

this is not any project, a security
conflict to be resolved. no working
paper, just working on paper,
nurturing the unsaid until it stops
                                        resisting.

i tell them i procrastinate, and i do.
oh, do i have a *crisis existencial* with Time,
but, she's irrelevant in writing verses.

"if i'm not on time, i'm not thriving,"
as if you're not drowning in the idea
of rowing your way around consumer
                                        behavior,

then landing, but not quite...
running, following around the supervisor
in your wrinkled white *camisas,*
impeccable black suit; i wear those too.

i'm proud too. i solve internal strife.

Acknowledgments

Thank you to the Creator Institute and Eric Koester, who built a community, making indispensable tools available to aspiring authors to achieve their dreams. For my editors, Scott Aronowitz and Kristin Gustafson, who worked tirelessly to give me the feedback I've been seeking for years.

Thank you to my incredible friends and mentors (shoutout to Grace Hasson), who introduced me to plenty timeless works and authors that have shaped classical and contemporary poetic thought.

Thank you to those who connected with me beyond surface-level conversations, and those who caught me off guard with unexpected emotions, teaching me more about myself and love.

Thank you to Prof. Elizabeth Pidek, who, the first time I met her, asked me if I was related to the Dominican poet and playwright Máximo Avilés Blonda, further sparking my curiosity in literature, and encouraging me to read between the lines of life.

Thank you to Prof. Han Mei Gan, who, in every step of the way, never ceased believing in my potential, and not only supported me with my academic endeavors (Monografía) but also extended her genuine affection and preoccupation for my growth and well-being, becoming way more than just a high school teacher.

Thank you to Pedro Cairo (rest in peace), who was extremely patient with me as I struggled through mathematics while I used poetry as an outlet during his class periods.

Thank you to Daniel Bosch, who I've been avoiding showing this collection for the fear of not fulfilling his expectations, and yet I'm deeply grateful for teaching me that most writing can be an experiment but only a few experiments can become poems.

Thank you to my parents, Wendy Alberty and Edwin Avilés, who trusted in me with every decision and exhorted me to take a step back to reflect and evaluate when needed, as well as reminding me to feel grateful and making me equipped with the confidence and assertiveness to become more independent and self-sufficient.

And, I am eternally thankful for each one of you who have been there all along--sharing, commenting, suggesting, donating, and overall dedicating time to help me keep evolving as a writer and a human. The following individuals made an additional financial effort to support me in the publishing journey, and fulfilling this dream would have not been possible without your cooperation:

María Laura García	Juan David Peralta
Mauro Veras	Jared Anwar
Edwin Avilés & Wendy Alberty	Pilar Rubio Beltrán
	Camila Gedanken

Eric Koester	Lisa Dyson
Ana-Natalia Epstein	Mildred Samboy
Natalia Ureña	Jorge Risk
Dana Diab	Emilie Lluberes
Neha Gundavarapu	Camila Giraldez
Alaín Perdomo	Emmanuel Goico
Francis Encarnación	Ana Cristina Pérez
Chuck Ofodike	Fabián Fidalgo
Daniel Carvajal	Genoveva Villanueva
Luis Ortíz & Gina Alberty	Dorca Mateo
Julián Peña	Haritz Echarren
Niharika Shah	Helen Griffith
Roberto Alberty & Teresa Rodríguez	Génesis Suazo
Ayah Noor Assaadi	Emma West
Danae Biscardi	Jessica Forsstrom
Fernanda Zavala	Kyung Jin Cho
Shreya Tibrewala	Aayush Gupta
Josette Goldar	Yamil Aristy
Elan Campos	Emilio Rosas Gutiérrez
Judy Dorrejo	Ethan Glickfield
Grace Wetsel	Manuel Alberty
Victor Santana	Anjelica Abraham
Anna Gómez	Dimitri Fernández
Isabella Johnson	Jafer Hasnain
Maiah Welle	Brennan Dyson
	Aldo Polanco

Giorgio Brunacci	Rafael Valdivieso
Hector Montes de Oca	Víctor Julián
Megan Yang	Javier Galán
Zone Li	Marcela Soto
Brian Mejía	Mehnaz Shafquat
Ashley Bostek	Ramón Contreras Díaz
Tenzin Tsering	Connor Clerkin
Efraín Tejeda	José Daniel Rodríguez
Kwame Armah	Adam Latif
Héctor Lora	Luis Jiménez
Gabriella Márquez	Dasom Lee
Ramón Ureña	Amy Ariza
Christian Bradley	Jesús Báez
Sandeep Reddy	Nicole Santana
Sophia Boraschi	Víctor Eduardo Gómez
Matthew Somekh	Clara Cao
Kara Swain	Mara Ríos Brache
Alicia Germán Dihmes	Daniel Hart
Lizzie Cohen	Simón de los Santos
Shreya Naik	Jean Carlos Fuentes
Valerie Cella	Amado Trinidad
Joel Pimentel	Jack Lewis
Miga Xie	Giancarlo Becattini
Zach Goldman	Jessalyn Arthur
Matthew Ortega	Ricardo Hernández
GianMarco Douglas	José Beltré Cuevas

Trinity Saxon	Yusuf Dougherty
Paola Pagán	Daniel Camejo
Justin January	Ivette Matos
Eduardo Santos	Nicole Melo
Alfonso Pimentel	Christa Sobon
John Charles Unser	Jesús Palenzuela
Iara Al-Schamma	Johanna Trigo
Mariah Mizbani	Layla Wofsy
Gisela Cifres	María Jesús Santana
Carlos Sanlley	Miguelina Feris
Diana Tejeda	Samuel Bonilla
Keaton Silver	Pelegrín Castillo
Arturo Féliz-Camilo	José Montes de Oca
Abi Nosrati	Isabela Jiménez
Sarah Kassabian	María González
Oscar Moquete	Paula Bonetti Tejeda
Jean García Periche	Mónica Geraldes
Wes Thompson	Zack Severino
Ash Shankar	Eduardo Guzmán
Maxwell Vore	Lia Silva
Derrick Tran	Miguel Alejandro Martínez
Andrea Seravalle	Valeria Martínez
Román Pimentel	Diana Pérez
Jesús Pérez	Julissa Astacio
Stalin Vargas	Yusr Zaghlula
Paula Luna	Roseliny Hidalgo

Claudia García	Rebecca Garner
Eddy Hugo Peralta	Caonabo Almonte
Zitlali Arrellano	Angel de los Santos
Federico Pagés	Luis Daniel Sosa
Ellie McAfee	Andrea González
Grace Hasson	Gabriel Casati
Bill Perdomo	Elizabeth Purnell
Raúl Lamarche	Miguel Carmona
Sócrates Álvarez	Mario Malagón
Rosa Fernández & Noel Ureña	Xiomara Martin
María José Chami	Mónica Aquino
Laura Herrera	Elvis Eusebio
Alexia García	Eliana Kavouriadis
Rosanna Álvarez	Ezequiel Genao
Lisa Oliva	Eduardo Avilés
Francisco Comas	Giuliano Rengifo
Carolina de Hostos	Daniel D'Meza
Genoveva Alba	China Dennington
Gabriela & Liah San Miguel	Rosanna Alberty
Melissa Messina	Vivian Fatule
Kashvi Golechha	Cahill Carusos
Delio Guzmán	Grecia Avilés
Sarah Wright	Ashley Hernández
Oscar Escobar	

Appendix

NOTE FROM THE AUTHOR

Flores, J. *Divided borders: Essays on Puerto Rican identity*. Houston, Tex: Arte Público Press, 1993.

Haugen, E. "Dialect, Language, Nation." *American Anthropologist, 68*(4), 922–935, 1966.

Ortiz, F. "Por la Integración Cubana de Blancos Y Negros." *Revista Estudios Afrocubanos*. La Habana, vol. 5. 1945-1946. pp. 222.225.

www.ingramcontent.com/pod-product-compliance
Lightning Source LLC
LaVergne TN
LVHW012033060526
838201LV00061B/4576